CALL YOUR LEADS.

101 TIPS TO IMPROVE SALES

(SEVERAL SALESPEOPLE WERE OFFENDED IN THE MAKING OF THIS BOOK)

MARSHALL MORRIS

Call Your Leads
ISBN 978-0-692-87364-9

Thrive Publishing
Published by Thrive Publishing
1100 Suite #100 Riverwalk Terrace
Jenks, OK 74037

Printed in the United States of America.

Thrive Publishing books may be purchased for educational, business or sales promotional use. For more information, please email founder@madness-media.com.

HOW TO USE THIS BOOK:

Sales managers for centuries have been puzzled by their sales team members that simply will not call their leads. A team member may be the best closer in the world, but picking up the phone and dialing seems to be a foreign language. This happens for many reasons, whether it be 1) a divine voice speaking to them to not do it, 2) mere laziness, 3) an exceptional case of Jackassery (see Clay Clark's *Jackassery*), 4) wealth repulsion activation system, or 5) lack of the *Call Your Leads* tips and guidance.

In this book, you will find countless (specifically 101) tips that will immediately improve your sales team's performance. Use this book much like a dinner party appetizer tray - pick and choose the tips that you feel are most applicable to you and your team. If something does not immediately resonate with you and your team, move on and come back to it at a later date. There is a tip for every sales team in this book, and you should feel free to marinate on each tip as long as necessary. Most tips are best applied regularly.

"People often say that motivation doesn't last. Well, neither does bathing - that's why we recommend it daily."
Zig Ziglar

If there is a particular tip that has a profound impact on you, or if you feel like somebody on your sales team needs to hear a tip to get them motivated, make sure you share this book with them. Anybody can be successful in sales if they follow these sales tips that have worked for centuries. My sincere interest is to help everyone to achieve the financial freedom they are looking for through sales, and it begins with calling your leads.

CHAPTER 1: The Basics

TIP #1:
Call your leads.

QUOTE

"I have always said that everyone is in sales. Maybe you don't hold the title of salesperson, but if the business you are in requires you to deal with people, you, my friend, are in sales."

-Zig Ziglar, American author, salesman, and motivational speaker

TIP #2:

After you have called your leads, call your leads.

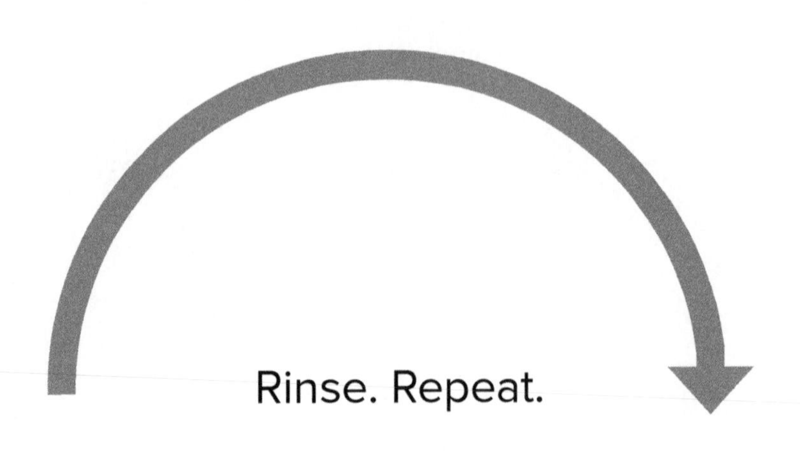

TIP #3:

Maybe your prospect's phone is off.
Text your leads.

TIP #4:

Maybe the phone number they gave you isn't working. Search their name, number, & email address on Facebook and call your leads.

TIP #5:

Maybe your prospect didn't pay his or her phone bill.

Email your leads.

TIP #6:
Use your sales script to call your leads.

No Script = No Sales

TIP #7:

1% training.
99% reminding.
Call your leads.
Just do it.
This is me
reminding you.

TIP #8:
Quit talking, go call your leads.

TIP #9:

Nobody likes making cold calls. Everyone likes money. With that being said, call your leads.

FUN FACT

"Buyers said that only 20% of sales people add value to the transaction. On the positive side, sales reps who were able to add value saw five times greater engagement with their potential buyers."
-*www.salesforce.com*

TIP #10:

When's your next appointment?

Until then, go call your leads.

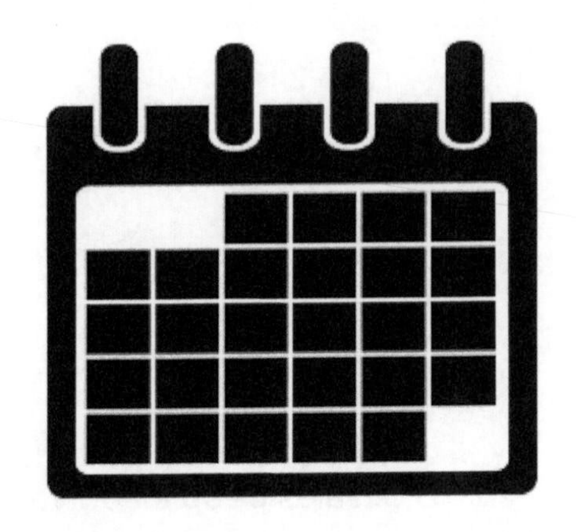

TIP #11:

Don’t have any appointments?

You should have been calling your leads. Go call your leads.

FUN FACT

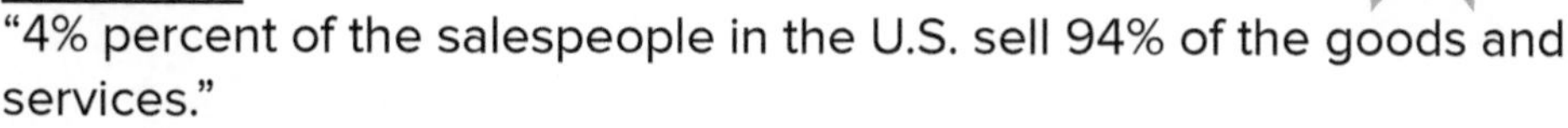

“4% percent of the salespeople in the U.S. sell 94% of the goods and services.”

-Harvard University and Gallup

TIP #12:

The path to financial freedom is to call your leads.

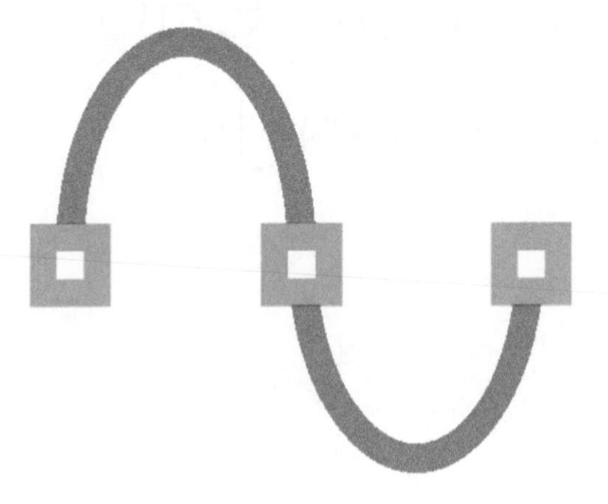

TIP #13:

Looking for a promotion?

Go call your leads.

FUN FACT

The best-paying state for sales managers: New York, where they earn $174,210 a year, on average.
-U.S. Bureau of Labor Statistics

TIP #14:

What should you do now?

Call your leads.

TIP #15:

"I think we should have a meeting abou.... nevermind, call your leads."

QUOTE

"Executives consider more than two-thirds (67 percent) of meetings to be failures."

"Failed meetings waste about $3.1 million every year."

-Rick Gilbert, *www.cnbc.com*

TIP #16:

Keep calm and call your leads.

TIP #17:

"I'm not telling you it will be easy, I'm telling you it's going to be worth it...until then call your leads."

QUOTE

"You don't have to be a genius or a visionary or even a college graduate to be successful. You just need a framework and a dream."

-Michael Dell, founder and CEO of Dell Technologies
(he called his leads)

TIP #18:

Want a raise?

Call your leads.

FUN FACT

"I don't think anyone deserves a raise just for showing up...If you've been at a company for three years, then expect a raise in the fourth year, why? If you want consistent raises, you have to keep learning and adding to your skillset all the time."
-businessinsider.com

TIP #19:

Stop making excuses and call your leads. Excuses are for losers.

FUN FACT

"Employees tend to run into some roadblocks more often than others. Traffic remains the most common reason employees say they're late (39 percent), followed by lack of sleep (19 percent), problems with public transportation (8 percent), bad weather (7 percent) and dropping the kids off at daycare or school (6 percent)."
-www.careerbuilder.com

TIP #20:

I’ve got a fever, and the only prescription is to call your leads.

TIP #21:

Yesterday is history, tomorrow is a mystery, today you get to call your leads.

ONE DAY AT A TIME.

TIP #22:

Leads are a lot like significant others. You should call your leads.

The leads ~~They~~ will love you.

TIP #v23:

Call your leads,
or somebody else will.

TIP #24:

When you feel like you're out of things to do, call your leads.

TIP #25:

Drink a nice warm glass of call your leads.

TIP #26:

Good things come to those who keep calling their leads.

QUOTE

"Patience is a virtue, and I'm learning patience. It's a tough lesson."

-Elon Musk, founder of PayPal, Tesla, and SpaceX

TIP #27:

You can do it.
Call your leads.

QUOTE

"People who are unable to motivate themselves must be content with mediocrity, no matter how impressive their other talents."

-Andrew Carnegie, one of the richest people and Americans ever.

TIP #28:

If your phone breaks, Facebook message your leads.

TIP #29:

In a post-apocalyptic world, send smoke signals to your leads.

TIP #30:

Smile and dial. Call your leads.

TIP #31:

Be encouraged. Call your leads.

QUOTE

"The way to develop self-confidence is to do the thing you fear and get a record of successful experiences behind you."

-William Jennings Bryan, American orator and politician, 3-time Democratic Party nominee for President of the United States

TIP #32:

You're not here to socialize. Call your leads.

FUN FACT

"With 24/7 connectivity, we face a growing time famine, where the pressure to get work done may eclipse the desire to socialize."
-www.nytimes.com

TIP #33:

If you just got hung up
on,
call your leads.

Stay Focused

1. Some Will
2. Some Won't
3. So What
4. Next!

TIP #34:

Looking to take a sick day?
Even if you don't feel well, call your leads.

FUN FACT

"If you called in sick to work during the last year even though you felt fine, you're not alone.

Thirty eight percent of U.S. employees did it — using such lame excuses as being stuck under a bed — according to an annual survey by CareerBuilder, the largest online job site in the U.S."
-*www.usatoday.com*

TIP #35:

The fastest path to driving a Bentley is by calling your leads.

TIP #36:

Want to be successful in pharmaceutical sales?
Call your leads.

TIP #37:

Want to build a business?
Then you need to call your leads.

TIP #38:

No time?
Make time to call your leads.

#noexcuses

TIP #39:

The trick to hitting your sales quota is to call your leads.

FUN FACT

"Your sales team has a 56% greater chance to attain quota if you engage buyers before they contact a seller."
-blog.hubspot.com

TIP #40:

Don't feel like calling your leads? Call your leads.

QUOTE

"You can't get much done in life if you only work on the days when you feel good."

-Jerry "The Logo" West, retired NBA basketball player

TIP #41:

The hardest part about calling your leads is starting to call your leads.

QUOTE

"The secret of getting ahead is getting started."

-Mark Twain, American writer, humorist, entrepreneur, publisher, and lecturer

TIP #42:

Before the end of the day,
call your leads.

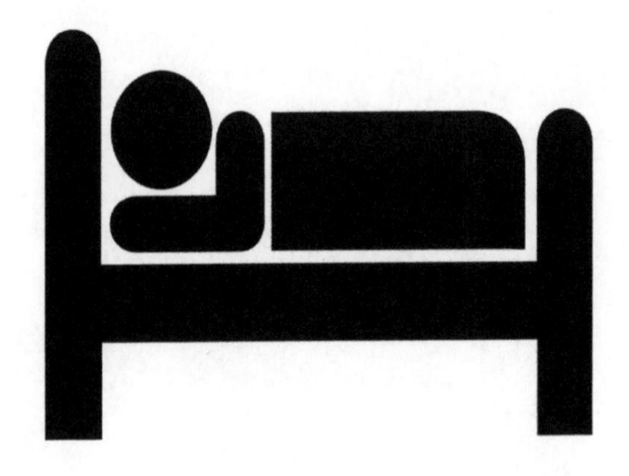

TIP #43:

Hell or high water, call your leads.

TIP #44:

The most important rule of sales is to call your leads.

TIP #45:

Be strategic. Call everyone.

TIP #46:

Want more time freedom? Call your leads.

CALLS = MONEY = TIME FREEDOM

TIP #47:

Having a bad day? The best remedy is to call your leads.

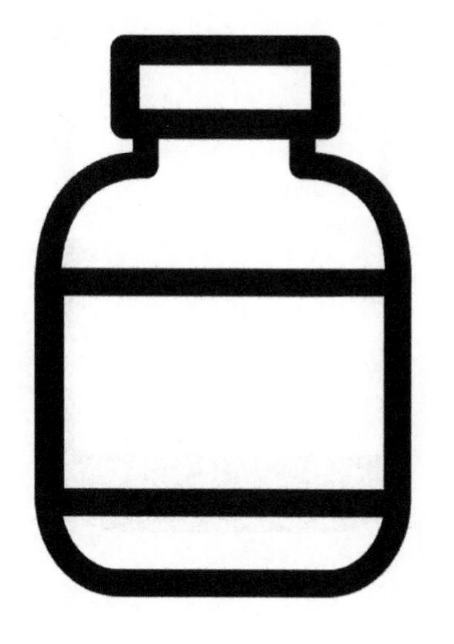

TIP #48:

Less Twitter. More “call your leads.”

TIP #49:

"I can't wait for tomorrow because you get to call your leads."

FUN FACT

"It takes 18 dials to connect with a single buyer."
-blog.hubspot.com

TIP #50:

It's the holidays! Celebrate by calling your leads.

CHAPTER 2: Expert Tips

TIP #51:

The meaning to life is to call your leads.

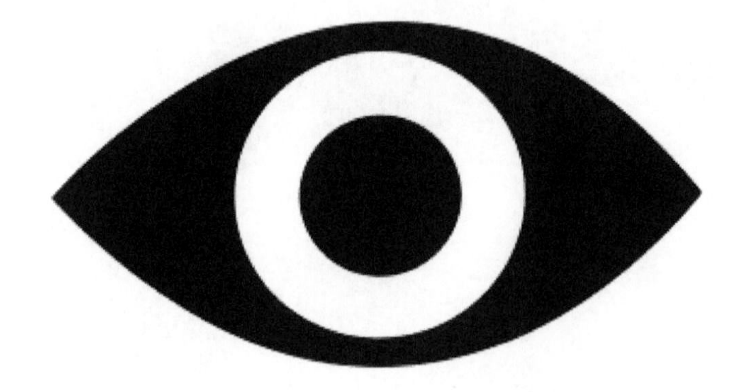

TIP #52:

Go buy a phone and call your leads.

FUN FACT
$19.99

Motorola Moto E Android Prepaid Phone with Triple Minutes (Tracfone)

https://www.amazon.com/Motorola-Android-Prepaid-Minutes-Tracfone/dp/B00PWEN2ZE/ref=sr_1_1?s=wireless&ie=UTF8&qid=1490820431&sr=1-1&keywords=pay+as+you+go+cell+phones

TIP #53:

Call. Your. Leads. How many times do we have to say it?

TIP #54:

Bottom line: call your leads.

FUN FACT

"Less than 25% of companies who receive a web lead will respond by phone."

-blog.hubspot.com

TIP #55:

If all else fails, call your leads. It's not hard.

QUOTE

"Without continual growth and progress, such words as improvement, achievement, and success have no meaning."

-Benjamin Franklin, one of the Founding Fathers of the United States

TIP #56:

The secret to success is to call your leads.

QUOTE

"There are no secrets to success. It is the result of preparation, hard work, and learning from failure."

-Colin Powell, retired four-star general in the United States Army

TIP #57:

This just in: call your leads. #newideasareweak

TIP #58:

WWJD?

Call your leads.

QUOTE

"The point is this: whoever sows sparingly will also reap sparingly, and whoever sows bountifully will also reap bountifully."

-2 Corinthians 9:6

TIP #59:

Let me make myself
clear,
call your leads.

TIP #60:

Do your job: call your leads.

TIP #61:

Live long, and prosper, and call your leads.

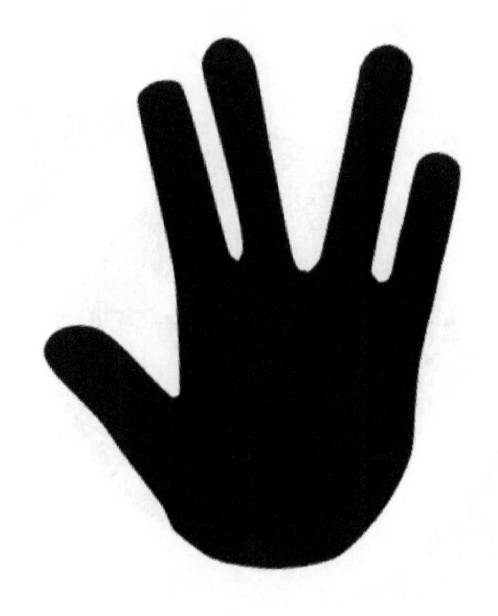

TIP #62:

Call until they buy, cry, or die.

TIP #63:

Get on the phone, and call your leads.

TIP #64:

Turn your leads into deals by calling your leads.

TIP #65:

Want to be the best? Start by calling your leads.

QUOTE

"There is no prize in sales for second place. It's win or nothing. The masters know this and strive for - they fight for - that winning edge."

-Jeffrey Gitomer, American author, professional speaker, and business trainer

TIP #66:

Want to become better at sales? Call your leads.

QUOTE

"Anyone who stops learning is old, whether at twenty or eighty. Anyone who keeps learning stays young."

–Henry Ford, founder of Ford Motor Company

TIP #67:

The key to sales is to call your leads. #itsnotrocketscience

TIP #68:

Beat your competition to the office to call your leads.

TIP #69:

Stop talking.
Get on the phone.
Call your leads.

QUOTE

"The way to get started is to quit talking and begin doing."

-Walt Disney, founder of Walt Disney World Resorts & pioneer of the American animation industry

TIP #70:

Did your client miss an appointment?
Call your leads.

TIP #71:

Have an extra 5 minutes? Call your leads.

TIP #72:

Don't be surprised when I say, "call your leads."

FUN FACT

"A clean desk helps you stick with a task more than one and a half times longer."

-Harvard Business Review

TIP #73:

You miss 100 percent of the appointments you don't set. Call your leads.

QUOTE

"Winners are not afraid of losing. But losers are. Failure is part of the process of success. People who avoid failure also avoid success."

-Robert T. Kiyosaki, author of *Rich Dad Poor Dad* (#1 personal finance book of all time)

TIP #74:

Insanity is doing the same thing over and over again expecting somebody else to call your leads.

QUOTE

"Failure isn't fatal, but failure to change might be"

-John Wooden, won ten NCAA national basketball championships in a 12-year period as head coach at UCLA

TIP #75:

Dream big. And call your leads.

QUOTE

"A dream doesn't become reality through magic; it takes sweat, determination and hard work."

-Colin Powell, retired four-star general in the United States Army

TIP #76:

Don't wait until you are motivated.
Call your leads, that will motivate you.

QUOTE

"Nothing is impossible. 'Impossible' just takes a few more phone calls."

-Michael J. Fox, Canadian-American actor, author, producer, and activist

TIP #77:

Just do it,
call your leads.

QUOTE

"If you're going through hell, keep going."

-Winston Churchill, Prime Minister of the United Kingdom when they stood up to Hitler

TIP #78:
Can you hear me now... calling your leads?

TIP #79:

Snap!
Crackle!
Pop!
Call your Leads!

QUOTE

"The top salesperson in the organization probably missed more sales than 90% of the sales people on the team, but they also made more calls than the others made."

-Zig Ziglar, American author, salesman, and motivational speaker

TIP #80:

When it rains, it pours. When you call your leads, you close deals.

TIP #81:

It's significantly more effective to book deals when you call your leads.

QUOTE

"Sales are contingent upon the attitude of the salesman - not the attitude of the prospect."

-W. Clement Stone, businessman, philanthropist and New Thought self-help book author

TIP #82:

Think different. Except for sales. Then just call your leads.

TIP #83:

Cell phone: The ultimate lead-calling machine. Use it.

TIP #84:

Quit looking at your phone waiting for inbound sales calls.

TIP #85:

I've developed a new social media platform called "call your leads."

FUN FACT

"One in 4 workers admitted that, during a typical workday, they will spend at least an hour on personal calls, emails, or texts."
-www.careerbuilder.com

TIP #86:

Wake up earlier and call your leads.

FUN FACT

"The early bird gets the worm. 50% of sales go to the first salesperson to contact the prospect."
-www.InsideSales.com

TIP #87:

ABC – Always be calling your leads.

FUN FACT

"80% of sales require 5 follow-up calls after the meeting. 44% of salespeople give up after 1 follow-up."
-www.marketingdonut.co.uk.com

TIP #88:

I have a secret...

#itsnosecret

TIP #89:

...next page...

QUOTE

"Obstacles are necessary for success because in selling, as in all careers of importance, victory comes only after many struggles and countless defeats."

--Og Mandino, author of *The Greatest Salesman in the World*

TIP #90:

...no, the next page...

(Flip faster.)

(Call faster.)

(Close faster.)

FUN FACT

"In 2007 it took an average of 3.68 cold call attempts to reach a prospect. Today it takes 8 attempts."

-*www.ovationsales.com*

TIP #91:

...call your leads.

FUN FACT

"The average salesperson only makes 2 attempts to reach a prospect."

-www.siriusdecisions.com

TIP #92:

Noise cancelling headphones or headsets tell people, "Leave me alone, I'm calling my leads."

TIP #93:

No one cares about your leads...only you do. So call your leads.

QUOTE

"Nobody cares how much you know, until they know how much you care."

-Theodore Roosevelt, 26th president of the United States and certified badass

TIP #94:

Turn off your notifications.
It will help you call your leads.

TIP #95:

You will not find time to call your leads. Just call your leads.

Here is a clock - time is already found.

TIP #96:

Do not go to bed until you call your leads.

QUOTE

"Beds are for the weak. I sleep standing up so I can call my leads."

-Steve Currington, owner of GetKoalified.com and proud owner of a Lamborghini

TIP #97:

You need a spiritual infusion of call your leads.

TIP #98:

Make sure you have it in your calendar this week to call your leads.

QUOTE

"Vision without execution is hallucination."

-Thomas Edison, American inventor and businessman, who has been described as America's greatest inventor

TIP #99:

"Hey boss, what should I be doin-..."

"Call your leads."

QUOTE

"As I grow older, I pay less attention to what men say. I just watch what they do."

-Andrew Carnegie, one of the richest people and Americans ever

TIP #100:

Can't sleep? Don't call your leads.

Take some Nyquil, then in the morning wake up and call your leads.

QUOTE

"If you really want to do something, you'll find a way. If you don't, you'll find an excuse."

–Jim Rohn, American entrepreneur, author and motivational speaker

TIP #101:

Call your leads.

QUOTE

"Success isn't a result of spontaneous combustion. You must set yourself on fire."

-Arnold H. Glasow, America business man who ran a humor magazine for 60 years

These tips have been researched and proven by a number of successful salesmen in a variety of industries including:

Marshall Morris - Thrive15.com Partner, co-author of *Start Here*, and founder of Madness-Media.com

Steve Currington - Partner at Total Lending Concepts who just bought a Lamborghini (GetKoalified.com & SteveCurrington.com)

Clay Clark - US Small Business Administration Entrepreneur of the Year and founder of Thrive15.com

Mickey Michalec - founder of Capital Waste Solutions & successful pharmaceutical sales representative who loves cold calling

Jonathan Kelly - manages advertising for 50+ clients with Make Your Life Epic and owner of TulsaFlipbooks.com

For more information, visit theworldsbestsalesbook.com or madness-media.com.

Follow Marshall Morris on Twitter @MarshallFMorris or email founder@madness-media.com.

CPSIA information can be obtained
at www.ICGtesting.com
Printed in the USA
BVHW011956150222
629109BV00007B/302